TULSA CITY-COUNTY LIBRARY

How Is a Pencil Made?

by Grace Hansen

Abdo Kids Jumbo is an Imprint of Abdo Kids
abdobooks.com

abdobooks.com

Published by Abdo Kids, a division of ABDO, P.O. Box 398166, Minneapolis, Minnesota 55439. Copyright © 2019 by Abdo Consulting Group, Inc. International copyrights reserved in all countries. No part of this book may be reproduced in any form without written permission from the publisher. Abdo Kids Jumbo™ is a trademark and logo of Abdo Kids.

102018
012019

 THIS BOOK CONTAINS RECYCLED MATERIALS

Photo Credits: Alamy, Getty Images, iStock, Shutterstock

Production Contributors: Teddy Borth, Jennie Forsberg, Grace Hansen

Design Contributors: Dorothy Toth, Laura Mitchell

Library of Congress Control Number: 2018945738
Publisher's Cataloging-in-Publication Data

Names: Hansen, Grace, author.
Title: How is a pencil made? / by Grace Hansen.
Description: Minneapolis, Minnesota : Abdo Kids, 2019 | Series: How is it made?
  Includes glossary, index and online resources (page 24).
Identifiers: ISBN 9781532181924 (lib. bdg.) | ISBN 9781532182907 (ebook) |
  ISBN 9781532183393 (Read-to-me ebook)
Subjects: LCSH: Pencils--Juvenile literature. | Manufacturing processes--Juvenile
  literature. | Pencil industry--Juvenile literature.
Classification: DDC 674.88--dc23

Table of Contents

Pencils 4

Making Pencils 10

The Final Product 20

More Facts 22

Glossary 23

Index 24

Abdo Kids Code 24

Pencils

It may be a small **utensil**, but it takes a lot of work to make a pencil!

Pencils are often made of cedar wood. Cedar is soft enough to be sharpened. But it is strong enough not to break while in use.

Pencil lead is not lead at all. It is a mixture of graphite and clay. The mixture is baked in an oven at about 1800 °F (982 °C).

Making Pencils

Cedar slats that are 5 mm thick pass under a cutting wheel. The wheel carves grooves into the wood. These grooves will hold the lead.

Another machine fills the grooves with glue. Earlier, the baked lead was **molded** into long, thin pieces. A lead laying machine drops the lead into the grooves.

Identical wooden slats are placed on top. The slats are then **compressed**. Once the glue dries, they are ready for the next step!

The slats are cut into pencils. The new pencils get about 4 coats of paint. Then they are painted with a clear lacquer.

The pencils then go through a stamping machine. A stamping machine can complete 500 pencils per minute!

The Final Product

A machine puts a metal ring on each pencil. An eraser is placed into the metal ring. The pencils are then boxed and shipped!

21

More Facts

- The word "pencil" comes from the Latin word penicillus. It means "little tail."

- One pencil has enough graphite to write about 45,000 words!

- The world's largest pencil is in Malaysia. It stands 65 feet (19.8 m) high!

Glossary

compress – to be pressed together to form a solid mass.

graphite – a soft, black or gray form of carbon.

lacquer – a liquid used on wood to protect it and make it shiny.

lead – a heavy and soft metal that has a gray color.

mold – to be worked into a certain shape or form.

utensil – a simple and useful tool.

Index

cedar wood 6, 10, 14

cutting wheel 10

eraser 20

glue 12, 14

lacquer 16

lead 8, 10, 12

lead laying machine 12

metal ring 20

oven 8

paint 16

shipping 20

stamping machine 18

Visit **abdokids.com** and use this code to access crafts, games, videos, and more!

Abdo Kids Code:
HHK1924